J
634.9   Greene, Carol
GR
        I can be a forest
        ranger

$12.60

DATE			MR 26 '01
JE 15 '91	JUN 14 '90	APR 01 '08	
JY 27 '91	DEC 01 '94	JL 10 '98	NY 04 '01
SE 4 '91	MAY 08 '95	AUG 19 '98	O 28 '01
OC 9 '91	JL 05 '95	OCT 20	JE 25 '02
MR 14 '92	JAN 02 '96	NOV 27	JY 29 '02
MR 26 '92	MAY 09 '96	JAN 12 '98	AG 05 '02
AP 20 '92	JAN 02 '98	MAR 08 '98	MY 1 '03
JY 10 '92	MAR 10 '97	AP 23 '99	JY 21 '03
AG 13 '92	JUN 25 '97	JY 07 '99	DE 04 '04
	JL 07 '97	JY 22 '99	JY 12 '05
MAR 3 '93	SEP 08 '97		JE 25 '06
MAR 30 '94	OCT 08 '97	JA 13 '00	AG 09 '08

© THE BAKER & TAYLOR CO.

I CAN BE A
FOREST RANGER

By Carol Greene

Prepared under the direction of Robert Hillerich, Ph.D.

CHILDRENS PRESS®

CHICAGO

Library of Congress Cataloging-in-Publication Data

Greene, Carol.
  I can be a forest ranger / by Carol Greene.
     p.   cm.
  Summary: Describes the duties and training of a forest ranger.
  ISBN 0-516-01924-4
  1. Forest rangers—Juvenile literature.   (1. Forest rangers.
2. Occupations.)   I. Title.
SD387.F6G74 1989   88-37717
634.9'023—dc 19   CIP
                                                              AC

PICTURE DICTIONARY

fuel

trees

forest

picnic area

wildlife

fire fighter

forest fire

lookout tower

rescue

campsite

forest ranger

visitors

trees

People have used trees for thousands of years. Very early people got food from fruit and nut trees. They burned wood to cook and keep warm. They made tools from wood. Some early people even lived in trees.

fuel

We still eat fruit and nuts. We use wood for fuel. We make things from wood.

Above: A forester checking on a tree's
condition
Right: Taking a "core sample" of a tree's trunk

But today there are
more people and fewer
trees. So we must do one
more thing. We must take
care of our trees.

People who do this job
are called foresters.

Above: A forester poisoning a tree that has a disease
Below: A healthy forest in the Adirondack Mountains of New York

Left: Rangers enjoy the beauty of our forestlands.
Right: A district ranger in the Blue Ridge Mountains of North Carolina

Foresters help other people to use forests better.

There are many kinds of foresters.

Some take care of a whole forest. They are called forest managers.

forest

8

District rangers study the problems in their section of a forest.

Some take care of part of a forest. They are called district rangers.

Some work mostly with wildlife. Others work with visitors to the forest.

All these people are often called forest rangers.

wildlife

visitors

forest ranger

Forest rangers want to keep their forests healthy. Trees can get diseases just as people can. Rangers watch out for these diseases.

Sometimes insects can harm trees. Rangers watch for harmful insects, too.

Fire can be a terrible
enemy to a forest. It kills
trees and animals.
Sometimes forest fires are
started by lightning. But
often careless people
start them.

forest fire

13

A fire lookout station in Mount Hood National Forest in Oregon

lookout tower

fire fighter

Forest rangers watch for fires. Some of them spend long hours in lookout towers. If a fire starts, they help fire fighters put it out. They also teach people to be more careful.

Above: A helicopter dropping water on a forest fire (left). Smokey the Bear reminds campers to be careful (right). Below: A lookout tower and firefighting rangers

It does not hurt a forest
to cut down trees. But
people must cut down the
right trees. And they must
not cut down too many.
Forest rangers decide
which trees can be cut.

Above: Hauling cut trees out of a forest. Below: Loading logs onto a truck (left).
A crane hoists logs onto a ship in Washington State for shipping overseas (right).

These young trees will one day grow into a tall forest.

Forest rangers also
decide where to plant
new trees. They show
other workers how to
plant them.

Planting new forest trees is called reforestation.
These pictures show some examples of how reforestation is done.

Raccoon

Elk bull

Of course, forests aren't just trees. Many kinds of animals live there, too. These animals need food and clean water. They need safe places to make their homes. Forest rangers make sure they have these things.

Elk cow

Lynx kitten

Black bear cubs

Doe with fawn triplets

Some forest rangers
even help make laws to
protect wildlife.

A deer drops in for dinner on a family camping trip.

Each year, many people visit forests. Some camp or go for hikes. Others fish or watch birds.

Forest rangers want visitors to have a good time. They make paths, picnic areas, and

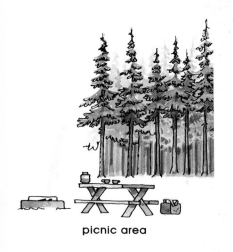

picnic area

People enjoy camping, hiking, fishing, and exploring in national forests and parks.

Left: Campers fixing dinner are careful not to start a forest fire.
Right: These campers are preparing a hearty breakfast beneath the trees.

campsite

rescue

campsites for them. They keep these places clean and safe.

But sometimes accidents happen. People get hurt or lost. Then forest rangers must rescue them.

Left: A ranger using a surveying instrument
Right: Tower Falls at Yellowstone Park in Wyoming

Most forest rangers go
to college for at least four
years. There they study
forestry. Others go to
special schools for one to
three years.

Park rangers giving a tour and helping an injured duck

Park rangers are different from forest rangers. Some park rangers work in forests. But they may work in many other places, too.

Left: A handicapped park ranger at Everglades National Park in Florida
Right: A ranger at the Vietnam War Memorial helps a visitor take a rubbing of a name.

A park ranger may take
care of a beach in Maine.
He or she may help visitors
at the Gateway Arch in
Saint Louis or at the
Vietnam War Memorial in
Washington, D.C.

27

Many people like to be outdoors. They like to work with plants and animals. They like to help other people enjoy nature, too.

Maybe that's why many people want to be forest rangers.

WORDS YOU SHOULD KNOW

accident (AK • sih • dent)—something harmful that happens by surprise or by mistake

beach (BEECH)—the sandy or rocky land that lies along an ocean, sea, or lake

campsite (KAMP • syt)—an outdoor area where people may camp

college (KAHL • ij)—a school where people can study after they finish high school

district ranger (DISS • trikt RAIN • jer)—a person who is in charge of part of a forest

forest manager (FOR • est MAN • i • jer)—a person who is in charge of a whole forest

forester (FOR • ess • ter)—a person who works with forests, trees, or wood products

forestry (FOR • ess • tree)—the science of forests and forest care

fuel (FYOO • ul)—a material that makes heat or power when it is burned

lookout tower (LOOK • out TAO • er)—a tall structure from which rangers watch for forest fires

rescue (RESS • kyoo)—to save from harm or danger

wildlife (WYLD • lyf)—birds, fish, and animals in their natural living areas

INDEX

ABOUT THE AUTHOR

Carol Greene has degrees in English literature and musicology. She has worked in international exchange programs, as an editor, and as a teacher. She now lives in Saint Louis, Missouri, and writes full time. She has published over seventy books for children. Others in this series include *I Can Be a Football Player*, *I Can Be a Baseball Player*, *I Can Be a Model*, and *I Can Be a Librarian*.